DUmbest Signs, aDs, and NeWSPaPeR HeaDLines

Compiled by the Editors at Tangerine Press

Illustrated and Designed by Dan Jankowski

Copyright© 2005 Scholastic Inc

Scholastic and Tangerine Press and associated logos are trademarks of Scholastic Inc

Published by Tangerine Press, an imprint of Scholastic Inc; 557 Broadway; New York, NY 10012

10 9 8 7 6 5 4 3 2 1

ISBN 0-439-80105-2

ROAD TRIP

WHAT DID THAT SIGN SAY?

Let's take a drive and see!

Rim Drive, Durango, CO

San Diego, CA

Boston, MA

Kyushi, Japan detour sign

A Street Downtown 1 MILE

BIG FOOT XING

Due to sightings in the area of a creature resembling "Big Foot" this sign has been posted for your safety.

CENTER OF THE WORLD

DANGER

EXPLOSIVE DELIVERIES ONLY

KEEP

RIGHT

CAUTION
WATER ON ROAD
DURING
RAIN

MOBI DITCH
BRIDGE

ENTRANCE
ONLY
DO NOT
ENTER

DIESEL FRIED CHICKEN

Wok & Roll

On the menu of a New Orleans restaurant:

Blackened bluefish

They have Mexican **FOOD.**

WE HAVE GAS!

in"JEAN"ious

POO PING
THAI CHINESE
CUISINE

WE SERVE
GRILLED
TIMBER WOLF

Kids With Gas Eat Free

In a Maine restaurant:

Open seven days a week
and weekends.

When this sign is under water, this road is impassable.

In a Los Angeles clothing store:

Wonderful bargains for men with
16 and 17 necks.

Istanbul hotel corridor sign:

Please to evacuate in hall especially
which is accompanied by rude noises.

Moscow hotel lobby across from a Russian Orthodox monastery:

You are welcome to visit the cemetery where famous Russian and Soviet composers, artists and writers are buried daily except Thursday.

Leipzig elevator:

Do not enter the lift backwards, and only when lit up.

Swiss mountain inn:

Special today—no ice cream.

BOGGUS MOTOR CO

Majorcan shop entrance:

English well talking.

On the door of a health food shop:

CLOSED DUE TO ILLNESS

Outside a muffler shop:

No appointment necessary.
We heard you coming.

On the door of a computer store:

Out for a quick byte.

On the door of a music library:

Bach in a min-u-et.

ELEPHANTS PLEASE STAY IN YOUR CAR

Spotted in a safari park

HORSE MANURE
$10 PER PRE-PACKED BAG
$1 DO-IT-YOURSELF

THE FARMER ALLOWS WALKERS TO CROSS THE FIELD FOR FREE, BUT THE BULL CHARGES.

On the door of a vet's office

Sit!
Be Back in
5
minutes.
Stay!

AUCTION
SUN NOV. 7 300PM
NEW AND USED FOOD

At a car towing company

WE DON'T CHARGE AN ARM AND A LEG. WE WANT TOWS.

JAW-JAH
PEACHES
5 FOR $2

At a roadside
stand in Georgia

Open, if I'm here.
Closed, if I'm not.

We repair what your husband fixed.

Copenhagen airline ticket office:
We take your bags and send them in all directions.

A sign on a restroom hand dryer
at O'Hare Field in Chicago

At a Santa Fe gas station:

We will sell gasoline to anyone in a glass container.

THIS WATER IS NOT FOR DRINKING.

In a cafeteria:

Shoes are required to eat in the cafeteria. Socks can eat any place they want.

In a Florida maternity ward:

No children allowed.

Toilet out
of order.
Please use
floor below.

In a Tacoma, Washington men's clothing store:

15 men's wool suits - $100 -
They won't last an hour!

If you cannot read, this leaflet will tell you how to get lessons.

On a roller coaster:
Watch your head.

**On an established
New Mexico dry cleaning store:**
Thirty-eight years on the same spot.

In a bowling alley:

PLEASE BE QUIET.
WE NEED TO
HEAR A PIN DROP.

Outside a country shop in West Virginia:

We buy junk and sell antiques.

Out to lunch;
if not back by five,
out for dinner.

QUICKSAND
Any person passing this
point will be drowned.
By order of the District Council.

Sign at the psychic's business:
Don't call us, we'll call you.

Bad Translations

Athens Hotel: Visitors are expected to complain at the office between the hours of 9 and 11 daily.

To move the cabin, push botton for wishing floor. If the cabin should enter more persons, each one should press a number of wishing floor. Driving is then going alphabetically by national order.

Hong Kong supermarket:

For your convenience, we recommend courageous, efficient self-service.

Japanese hotel room

Please to bathe inside the tub.

Moscow hotel room door:

If this is your first visit to Russia, you are welcome to it.

Is forbidden to steal hotel towels please. If you are not person to do such thing is please not to read this notice.

Tokyo hotel

A hair product company introduced the "Mist Stick," a curling iron, in Germany only to find out that "mist" is slang for manure. Not too many people had use for the "manure stick."

When an American baby food company started selling baby food in Africa, they used the same packaging as in the U.S., with a picture of a baby on the label. Later, they learned that in Africa, companies routinely put pictures on the label of what's inside, because most people can't read. People were disgusted that a company would sell ground up baby in a jar.

Pepsi's "Come alive with the Pepsi Generation" translated into "Pepsi brings your ancestors back from the dead," in Chinese.

The name Coca-Cola in China was first rendered as Ke-kou-ke-la. Unfortunately, the Coke company did not discover until after thousands of signs had been printed that the phrase means "bite the wax tadpole" or "female horse stuffed with wax" depending on the dialect. Coke then researched 40,000 Chinese characters and found a close phonetic equivalent, "ko-kou-ko-le," which can be loosely translated as "happiness in the mouth."

Also in Chinese, the Kentucky Fried Chicken slogan "finger-lickin' good" came out as "eat your fingers off."

When General Motors introduced the Chevy Nova in South America, it was apparently unaware that "no va" means "it won't go." The company renamed the car Caribe in its Spanish markets.

CLASSIFIED ADS

1985 Camaro red. 68,000 miles, runs good, needs motor.

FOR SALE
One pair hardly used dentures, only 2 teeth missing. $100

Men wanted to work in dynamite factory. Must be able to travel.

Turkey for sale.
Only partially eaten. Only 8 days old. Both drumsticks still intact. $23

Wanted: Somebody to go back in time with. This is not a joke. You will get paid when get back.

Main Street Pizza.
We deliver or pick up.

Dinner Special—
Turkey $2.35;
Chicken or Beef $2.25;
Children $2.00

Now is your chance to have your ears pierced and get an extra pair to take home, too.

Housing two bedroom sublease, nice area, BARGAIN rent. Drawback: big hairy spiders drop off ceiling at night.

Stock up and save. Limit one.

Get rid of aunts: Zap does the job in 24 hours.

Two-pound Lab puppies. Call and leave mess.

Wanted: Free furniture, bedding, kitchen table, color TV, etc.

Three-year-old teacher needed for preschool. Experience preferred.

For Sale: Parachute, never opened, used once.

Tired of working for only $9.25 an hour? We offer full benefits and flexible hours. Starting pay anywhere from $7 to $9 per hour.

Found:
Scraggly white dog, looks like a rat. There better be a reward.

Eight-year-old German Shorthaired Pointer.
Has all shots, speaks German, free.

Free dog. Eats anything,
and is fond of children

Queen-sized mattress.
Like new. Ten-year warranty,
minor urine smell.

Debbie's Hair Salon:
If we can't make you look
good, you're UGLY!

Illiterate? Write today for free help.

For Sale: One used tombstone. Perfect for anyone named Michael Smith.

TICKLE ME ELMO, STILL IN BOX, COMES WITH ITS OWN 1988 MUSTANG, 5L, AUTO, EXCELLENT CONDITION $6800

For Sale: 16-volume encyclopedias, not needed anymore because I know everything.

SNOW BLOWER FOR SALE... ONLY USED ON SNOWY DAYS.

Product Warnings

Air Conditioner

CAUTION

Avoid dropping
air conditioner
out of window.

Blow Dryer

WARNING

Do not use
while sleeping.

Iron

Never iron clothes on the body.

Vacuum Cleaner

1. Do not use to pick up gasoline or flammable liquids.
2. Do not use to pick up anything that is currently burning.

Life Saving Device

WARNING

This is NOT a life saving device!!!

Can of Soda

Contents under pressure. Cap may blow off causing eye or other serious injury. Point away from face and people, especially when opening.

**Child-Sized
Superman
Costume**

WARNING

**Wearing of this garment
does not enable you to fly.**

Camera

WARNING

**This camera will only
work when film is inside.**

WARNING

**Do not attempt to stick
head inside deck, which
may result in injury.**

**Video Game
Instruction Manual**

Toilet Cleaner

Safe to use around pets and children, although it is not recommended that either be permitted to drink from toilet.

Window Cleaner

Do not spray in eyes.

On a Bar of Soap

Directions:
Use like regular soap.

**On a hotel-provided
shower cap**

Fits one head.

**For indoor or
outdoor use only.**

String of
Christmas Lights

On a jar of peanuts

WARNING

Use repeatedly for severe damage

Bottle of Shampoo

On a Blanket

WARNING

Not to be used as protection from a tornado

Infant's Bathtub

WARNING

Do not throw baby out with bath water.

WARNING

This product contains small granules under 3 millimeters. Not suitable for children under the age of 14 years in Europe or 8 years in the USA.

Packet of Juggling Balls

INDUSTRIAL INSECT SPRAY

"Kills all kinds of insects!"

WARNING

This spray is harmful to bees.

Can of Insect Spray

Wheelbarrow

WARNING

Do not use when temperature exceeds 140° Farenheit.

Crazy Bumper Stickers

Buckle up! It makes it harder for the aliens to suck you from your car.

So, when's the wizard going to get back to you about that brain?

Don't eat the yellow snow!

Never

kick a fresh turd on a hot day.

Don't make me get my
flying monkeys!

Be kind to animals.
Hug a hockey player.

Do not meddle in the affairs of dragons.
For you are crunchy and good with ketchup.

One by One the Penguins Steal My Sanity.

I drive the speed limit.
If you don't like it, call a cop!

Cats are dogs
with a college education.

Sorry, I just haven't been the same
since that house fell on my sister.

Honk if you're illiterate

Out of my mind.
Be back in 15 minutes.

CELEBRATE
WHIRLED PEAS

Take your time, but hurry.

I love kids, but I can't eat a whole one.

HIRE TEENAGERS WHILE THEY STILL KNOW EVERYTHING!

If I roll up my windows and lock the doors, it's because you smell bad.

Change is inevitable...

Except for vending machines.

Of course you're faster, but I'm driving in front of you.

If you can't stop when I do,
smile as you go under!

Bright red meat is good for you,
Fuzzy green meat is not good for you.

There are only 2 choices on the menu:
Take it or Leave it.

Is that your head or did your neck throw up?

Car will explode upon impact

It's not how you pick your nose,
it's where you put the boogers.

Newspaper Headlines

Something Went Wrong in Jet Crash Experts Say

Police Begin Campaign To Run Down Jaywalkers

IF STRIKE ISN'T SETTLED QUICKLY, IT MAY LAST AWHILE

Two Sisters Reunited after 18 Years in Checkout Counter

British Left Waffles
on Falkland Islands

Blah Blah Blah Blah
Blah Blah Blah Blah
Blah Blah Blah Blah
Blah Blah Blah Blah
Blah Blah Blah Blah
Blah Blah Blah Blah

Iraqi Head Seeks Arms

Blah Blah Blah Blah
Blah Blah Blah Blah
Blah Blah Blah Blah
Blah Blah Blah Blah
Blah Blah Blah Blah
Blah Blah Blah Blah

Miners Refuse to Work after Death

ENRAGED COW INJURES FARMER WITH AX

Man Struck by Lightning Faces Battery Charge

Typhoon Rips Through Cemetery, Hundreds Dead

Survivor of Siamese Twins Joins Parents

Include Your Children When Baking Cookies

Drunk Gets Nine Months in Violin Case

Bridge Held Up By Red Tape

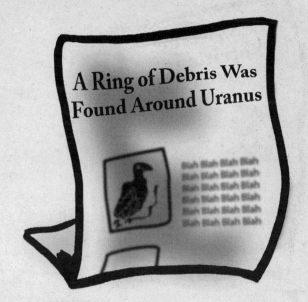

Kids Make Nutritious Snacks

Hospitals Sued By Seven Foot Doctors

Lawmen From Mexico Barbecue Guests

Nicaragua Sets Goal to Wipe Out Literacy

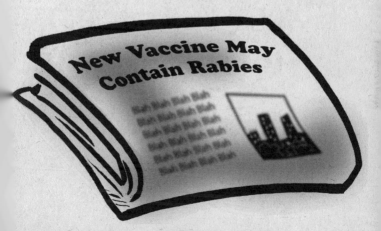

Wacky Town Names

Welcome to
BEST, TEXAS

CHRISTMAS,
FLORIDA

You just missed
CAREFREE,
ARIZONA

Come Back to
Celebration,
Florida

One mile to
Bountiful,
Utah

Thanks for Visiting
OKAY, OKLAHOMA

City Limits
Friendly, West Virginia

YOU'RE IN HAPPY CAMP CALIFORNIA

IDEAL, Georgia one mile away

HAPPYLAND CONNECTICUT

Welcome to
Lovely, Kentucky

Smileyberg,
Kansas

PARADISE,
MISSOURI
THREE MILES

Thanks for Visiting
MAGIC CITY,
INDIANA

Entering
**SUCCESS,
MISSOURI**

You just missed
**What Cheer,
Iowa**

WHYNOT,
NORTH CAROLINA

Welcome to
Boring,
Oregon

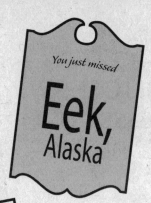

You just missed
Eek,
Alaska

GREASY,
OKLAHOMA

FLAT,
Texas
*Come Back
And See Us!*

GRIPE,
ARIZONA
2 MILES

Welcome to
HARDSCRABBLE, DELAWARE

Entering
Looneyville, TEXAS

One mile
ODDVILLE, Kentucky

City Limits
DINKYTOWN, Minnesota

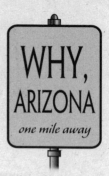

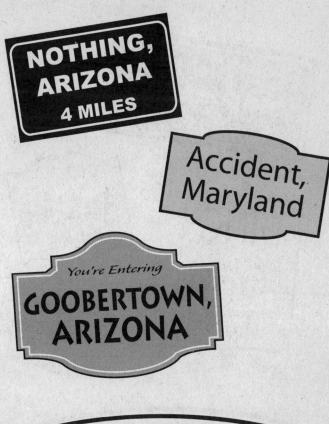

NOTHING, ARIZONA
4 MILES

Accident,
Maryland

You're Entering
GOOBERTOWN,
ARIZONA

Thanks for Visiting!
Wimp, California

LAST CHANCE,
COLORADO
5 MILES

DING
DONG,
TEXAS

You just missed
Accident,
Maryland

Frankenstein,
Missouri

Welcome to
Unalaska, Alaska

You just missed
CHEESEQUAKE, NEW JERSEY

One mile
BACON COUNTY, GEORGIA

MEAT CAMP, NORTH CAROLINA

THANKS FOR VISITING
BUTTERMILK, KANSAS

Welcome to
BURNT CORN, ALABAMA

CHOCOLATE BAYOU, TEXAS 1 MILE

SPUDS, FLORIDA one mile away

You just missed **TEA,** SOUTH DAKOTA

Ham Lake, Minnesota

MASHPEE,
MASSACHUSETTS

LICKSKILLET,
OHIO

Welcome to
LICK FORK,
VIRGINIA

You just missed
HOT
COFFEE,
Mississippi

PIE TOWN,
NEW MEXICO
8 MILES

Welcome to
Oatmeal,
Texas

You just missed
Picnic,
Florida

Thanks for Visiting
Oniontown,
Pennsylvania

SANDWICH, MASSACHUSETTS

You're Entering
Two Egg, Florida

One mile
Sugar City, IDAHO

You just missed
Tortilla Flat, Arizona

BELCHERTOWN, MASSACHUETTS

Beebeetown, Iowa

welcome to **BUGSCUFFLE, TENNESSEE**

Come Back Soon!
Gassville, Arkansas

Welcome to
Beaverdale
Pennsylvania

GOOSE PIMPLE JUNCTION, VIRGINIA
8 MILES

City Limits
Shoofly,
North Carolina

You just missed
Bear,
Delaware

BIRD-IN-HAND,
PENNSYLVANIA
10 MILES

BEAVER,
OKLAHOMA

BIRDSEYE,
INDIANA
Five miles away

You just missed
Elephant Butte,
New Mexico

Come back soon!
Dinosaur, Colorado

FISH HAVEN, IDAHO

HORSEHEADS, NEW YORK 5 MILES

CITY LIMITS MAMMOTH, WEST VIRGINIA

One Mile Ahead
Monkey's Eyebrow, Kentucky

Entering
Hungry Horse, Montana

Possum Trot, Kentucky

Rabbit Hash, Kentucky

You just missed

RABBIT SHUFFLE,

North Carolina

Welcome to

Squirrel Hill, Pennsylvania

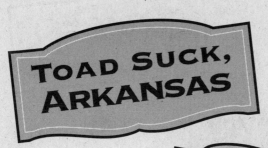

TOAD SUCK, ARKANSAS

Parrot, Kentucky

Entering **VIPER, KENTUCKY**

One more mile until **Trout, Louisiana**

CHICKEN, ALASKA

TURKEY, Texas

one mile away

Come back soon! BUZZARDS BAY, Massachusetts

TURKEY SCRATCH, ARKANSAS 1 MILE

STIFFKNEE KNOB, NORTH CAROLINA

Welcome to
Sweet Lips,
Tennessee

West
Thumb,
WYOMING

Come back soon!

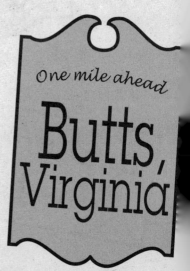

One mile ahead

Butts,
Virginia